Horses that Help

with the American Humane Association

The nation's voice for the protection of children...

THERAPY
HORSES THAT HEAL

Loren
Spiotta-DiMare

Enslow Elementary

The **Horses That Help** *series is dedicated to my sister, Sheryl, and niece, Katherine. We are so lucky to have each other and horses in our lives. I'd also like to extend a special thank you to Rozina Smith for contributing so many beautiful photographs to the series.* —Loren Spiotta-DiMare

American Humane Association™

The nation's voice for the protection of children & animals™

Since 1877, American Humane Association has been at the forefront of virtually every major advance in protecting children, pets, and farm animals from cruelty, abuse, and neglect. Today we're also leading the way in understanding the human-animal bond and its role in therapy, medicine, and society. American Humane Association reaches millions of people every day through groundbreaking research, education, training, and services that span a wide network of organizations, agencies, and businesses. You can help make a difference, too. Visit www.americanhumane.org today, call 1-866-242-1877, or write to American Humane Association at 1400 16th Street NW, Suite 360, Washington, DC 20036.

Enslow Elementary, an imprint of Enslow Publishers, Inc.

Enslow Elementary® is a registered trademark of Enslow Publishers, Inc.

Library of Congress Cataloging-in-Publication Data

Spiotta-DiMare, Loren.
   Therapy horses : horses that heal / Loren Spiotta-DiMare.
      pages cm. — (Horses that help with the American Humane Association)
   Audience: 8–up.
   Audience: Grade 4 to 6.
   Summary: "Opens with a true story about a young girl and her bond with therapy horses and follows with the history of therapy horses, what breeds are used, the training involved, what the horses do on the job, and what happens to therapy horses when they retire"— Provided by publisher.
   Includes bibliographical references and index.
   ISBN 978-0-7660-4217-9
   1. Horses—Therapeutic use—Juvenile literature. 2. Horsemanship—Therapeutic use—Juvenile literature. 3. Horses—Psychological aspects—Juvenile literature. 4. Human-animal relationships—Juvenile literature. I. Title. II. Title: Horses that heal.
   RC489.H67S65 2014
   615.8'51581—dc23
                           2012051306

Future editions:
Paperback ISBN: 978-1-4644-0377-4
EPUB ISBN: 978-1-4645-1208-7
Single-User PDF ISBN: 978-1-4646-1208-4
Multi-User PDF ISBN: 978-0-7660-5840-8

Printed in the United States of America

102013 Lake Book Manufacturing, Inc., Melrose Park, IL

10 9 8 7 6 5 4 3 2 1

To Our Readers: We have done our best to make sure all Internet addresses in this book were active and appropriate when we went to press. However, the author and the publisher have no control over and assume no liability for the material available on those Internet sites or on other Web sites they may link to. Any comments or suggestions can be sent by e-mail to comments@enslow.com or to the address on the back cover.

♻ Enslow Publishers, Inc., is committed to printing our books on recycled paper. The paper in every book contains 10% to 30% post-consumer waste (PCW). The cover board on the outside of each book contains 100% PCW. Our goal is to do our part to help young people and the environment too!

Every effort has been made to locate all copyright holders of material used in this book. If any errors or omissions have occurred, corrections will be made in future editions.

Photo Credits: Daniel Aguilar/Reuters/Landov, p. 42; AP Images/Topeka Capital-Journal, Angela Deines, p. 35; AP Images/ Pat Wellenbach, p. 12; © 1999 Artville, LLC, p. 19; Hemera/Thinkstock, p. 11; © Martin Kavanagh, p. 17; © Mane Stream, p. 29; Shutterstock.com, pp. 1 (horse head clipart), 3, 18, 23, 32, 43; Anne Marie J. Sima, p. 6; © Rozina Smith, pp. 1, 7, 8, 20, 26, 28, 33, 37, 39; © Craig Sotres, pp. 4, 10, 14, 16, 22, 30, 34, 41.

Cover Photo: © Rozina Smith (Michelle with Elwood); Shutterstock.com (horse head clipart).

CONTENTS

Michelle: A True Story

Horses are large, beautiful animals that are fun to ride. Some people enjoy trail riding. Others like to compete in horse shows. But you do not need to own a horse to enjoy them. Many people start out by taking riding lessons.

When Michelle was five years old, she joined a program at Mane Stream, a therapeutic riding center in New Jersey. Michelle has special needs, so her mother thought learning to ride would be a good form of exercise to strengthen Michelle's body. During a lesson, an instructor gave Michelle directions while a volunteer guided her horse using a lead line, which is like a dog leash. Two volunteer side walkers stayed on either side of Michelle to make sure she would not fall off.

This type of program is called adaptive riding at Mane Stream. It means the person moves the horse. Students, also called participants, ride as independently as they are able with their special needs. They are giving the horses directions with their legs, hands, and voices just like any other rider. Program participants are taught to move with their horses as they walk, trot, canter, and sometimes even jump. Trotting is almost like human jogging. Cantering is faster than trotting but slower than galloping, a horse's fastest speed.

In time, Michelle became strong enough to ride without the horse leader. She loved being around horses, and she also became very fond of Bob, one of her side walkers. She still remembers him, more than fifteen years later.

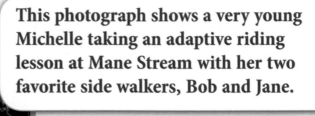

This photograph shows a very young Michelle taking an adaptive riding lesson at Mane Stream with her two favorite side walkers, Bob and Jane.

"I think one of the most important parts of therapeutic riding for Michelle was the compassion shown by the people involved and the horses themselves," Michelle's mother says. Riding did help Michelle strengthen her muscles and balance. And with her small group lessons, she was also able to enjoy a wonderful activity with other children.

Although Michelle was involved in art, dance, swimming, and yoga classes at the time, riding was her favorite activity. She is especially proud to have received an award for "Exceptional Performance in Vocal Commands and Trail Riding."

As an adult, Michelle takes lessons on the author's quarter horse, Elwood. "Michelle has wonderful posture and balance and keeps her heels down in the stirrups as riders should," says Michelle's riding instructor, Tiffany. "She loves to ride Elwood and has a special relationship with him."

As an adult, Michelle now takes private riding lessons. Her riding instructor, Tiffany, walks beside her.

Michelle has developed a special bond with the author's horse, Elwood.

Elwood likes Michelle too. He can be stubborn with some riders but is usually well behaved for Michelle. She calls him Cutie. But if Elwood starts being lazy and stops moving, Michelle says, "Elwood, don't be silly," gives him a vocal command, and gets him walking or trotting again.

Chapter 1

The History of Therapy Horses

People with disabilities have been horseback riding for centuries. In the early 1900s, the idea of including horses in physical-therapy programs developed in Europe. In 1969, the Professional Association of Therapeutic Horsemanship International (PATH Intl.) was founded in the United States under a different name. PATH supports horse-assisted activities and therapies for people with special needs around the world.

The earliest mention of using horseback riding to help people heal came from ancient Greece. Thousands of years ago, the ancient Greek doctor Hippocrates (Hip-pah-cruh-teez) wrote about riding a horse as exercise.

Spending time with horses is a wonderful experience for anyone, but it is especially helpful for those with physical challenges. For example, people with health problems that affect the spine, nerves, muscles, or brain can benefit greatly by participating in horse-related activities. Being on the backs of these large animals in motion moves a person's body in a way that is similar to how we walk, so it can strengthen muscles and improve balance, posture, and flexibility. Those who are unable to mount a horse can participate in carriage driving, where they drive horse-drawn carts. This activity also helps strengthen the body and gives the driver a unique sense of accomplishment.

This man is carriage driving at a therapeutic riding center in Maine. It is part of his physical and occupational therapy to strengthen his hands and fingers.

Therapy horses also help people deal with emotional problems, such as depression. When someone is depressed, he or she feels sad all the time. Participants in PATH programs form a special bond with horses. Over time, becoming friends with these beautiful, kind animals makes people feel better about themselves and their lives.

Chapter 2

Therapy Horse Breeds

Almost all horse breeds can be therapy horses as long as they are friendly and calm. They should not spook, or spin and run away, if something unexpected happens—for example, if a loud noise goes off. Therapy horses need to ignore wheelchairs, crutches, or objects that may be used in lessons. Another important trait for a therapy horse is how he walks. He must move in a way that is comfortable and helpful to the rider.

Horses are measured in hands from their hooves to their withers, which is at the top of the shoulders, below the neck. A hand equals four inches. Quarter horses, Thoroughbreds, Haflingers, and Norwegian Fjords are breeds that can be very good therapy horses.

Quarter Horses

Quarter horses stand between fourteen and sixteen hands (fifty-six and sixty-four inches). They are found in all colors. Sorrel is the most common. It is a reddish brown with a golden mane and tail. Many sorrels also have white markings on their faces and legs. Quarter horses are smart, willing, people-friendly, and calm.

Thoroughbreds

Thoroughbreds are tall, sleek, and lean. They are bred for speed. Many are racehorses, while others compete in different equine sports, such as jumping. (*Equine* is another name for a horse.) They are usually fifteen and

The author's horse, Elwood, is a sorrel quarter horse.

a half to seventeen hands (sixty-two to sixty-eight inches) in height. Most are bay (brown with a black mane and tail), chestnut (a reddish brown body, mane, and tail), black, or gray. They can also have white on their faces and legs. Some can be very high-spirited, but others are calmer and make great therapy horses.

This rider takes a jump riding her Thoroughbred sidesaddle. Sidesaddle means the person rides the horse with both legs on one side.

Haflingers

Haflingers are small draft horses, heavy breeds originally used for farmwork, such as plowing. Haflingers are usually between thirteen and a half and fifteen hands (fifty-four and sixty inches). They are always a golden color from a light brown to yellow with a flaxen, or golden white, mane. Even though they are smaller than many riding breeds, they are strong enough to carry adults and children. Some people may feel safer on Haflingers because they are not as high off the ground. These horses also have wonderful personalities. They are happy horses that really enjoy being with people, and they have a very good attitude toward working.

The Haflinger is a small draft horse with a golden coat and light mane and tail.

The name *Haflinger* comes from the village of Hafling, which today is in northern Italy. In the 1800s, farmers only had narrow, rocky paths to reach different villages. Haflingers were able to move through these trails easily, so they were used for transportation.

Norwegian Fjords

Like Haflingers, Norwegian Fjords are small draft horses. Standing between thirteen and fourteen and a half hands (fifty-two and fifty-eight inches), the Fjord has a very interesting appearance. Its body is dun, a sandy gold color, with a dark stripe along the back.

The rough mane, which stands up straight, is clipped so the black hairs in the center are higher than the outer silver hairs. The tail is usually silver too, and some horses have zebra markings on their lower legs. Fjords have calm personalities, so they are especially good for beginner riders. They are also excellent carriage-driving horses.

Norwegian Fjords are unique-looking horses. Their manes are black in the middle and silver on the sides.

It takes special horses to become therapy horses. They must be healthy, strong, and gentle. Many therapy horses have had other careers before they are given to or purchased by therapeutic riding centers. Former lesson, trail, show, driving, and police horses often make wonderful therapy horses.

Chapter 3

Therapy Horses on the Job

Therapy horses take part in many different kinds of programs. Remember, adaptive riding is when the person moves the horse. In equine-assisted therapy, the horse moves the person. Activities can also be performed on the ground. For example, grooming, placing the riding equipment on the horse (tacking up), and leading the horse help the participant's coordination and teach him or her to do things in proper order.

When Amelia arrived at Mane Stream, doctors had told her parents she would never walk. But as a result of the therapy, she did start walking! "After one particular session, Amelia simply stood up from her chair for the first time ever—all by herself," says Ruth, her physical therapist. "After another session, she took her first steps. Now all she wants to do is walk!"

Ten-year-old Richard became involved with equine-assisted therapy because he did not have much energy and his posture was weak. Because he was always uncomfortable, he could not join other boys in sports.

FAST FACT

Equine-assisted therapy was once called hippotherapy. *Hippos* means "horse" in Greek.

Working with his physical therapist and a Norwegian Fjord named Minnie gave Richard an activity he could enjoy without pain. At the same time, it improved his energy and strength.

In just more than a year, Richard improved so much that he was able to move out of the equine-assisted therapy program and into adaptive riding. He has become a talented horseback rider, and one day he hopes to even compete in horse shows.

Volunteers are a big part of therapeutic riding programs. Aside from side walkers, some volunteers are responsible for grooming and tacking up the horses before each lesson. Others lead the horses, assist with mounting, or set up courses.

Annette has been a volunteer for sixteen years. "The biggest joy is to see people who have multiple challenges grow into confident riders and some even can start to ride on their own," Annette says. "There is also the bond that develops between the horse and rider. Some students, who cannot communicate, hold on to the reins or horse when leaving. Others ask to take them home. For some students, this riding experience is the only time they are not in a wheelchair or using a walker. They are free on the back of a horse!"

Seven-year-old Audrey participates in speech therapy and occupational therapy. Some people have an illness, injury, or disability that makes doing everyday tasks difficult. For example, they have trouble getting dressed, taking a shower, or brushing their teeth. Occupational therapy helps them do these things.

Audrey has difficulty speaking and learning new things. She loves animals but is also a little bit afraid of them. Her mother, Lisa, thought introducing Audrey to equine-assisted therapy would not only improve her speech and build her muscles, but also help her overcome her fear. It worked!

Many people help Audrey as she engages in equine-assisted therapy. The long liner walks behind Alvin, the pony. The header is slightly in front of Alvin. The side walker walks on the right of Audrey, and her speech therapist is on her left, holding the laptop.

"Audrey loves Alvin, the pony she rides," her mother says. "She does not even feel like she is working on basic skills." Audrey's core, the center of her body, is weak, so much of her therapy focuses on improving her strength in this area. She has learned to trust Alvin, and her confidence has improved. "She is doing things on Alvin I never thought she would," her mother continues. "Like letting go and reaching up with both hands, laying all the way back, reaching forward and petting his mane. All of this while working on speech!"

Carriage driving and interactive vaulting are two other programs offered at Mane Stream. They provide a different kind of activity with a horse. The challenge of working together with a horse and learning an equine skill step-by-step helps the participant become more confident. The enjoyment he or she feels from learning to drive a carriage often encourages the participant to try other tasks and activities.

In interactive vaulting, movements are around, on, and off the horse. As participants get better at the tasks, they perform gymnastic positions on the horses as they walk, trot, and canter. For example, a participant may first learn how to kneel or stand on a horse while it is moving. After a lot of practice, he could eventually learn to balance on the moving horse with one knee on the saddle and the other leg in the air behind him.

Audrey works with her speech therapist, Angela. The way Alvin moves helps get Audrey's brain and muscles ready for speaking. Being on Alvin also helps her relax and have fun during speech therapy.

This participant does interactive vaulting on a Norwegian Fjord. This move is called the "prince."

"The appeal of an interactive vaulting class is that the vaulter can progress at his or her own speed while still being part of a group working together. The class is planned to encourage teamwork, to discover and practice new skills, and to have fun," explains Gina, an occupational therapist.

Training Therapy Horses

There are many types of professionals involved in equine-assisted therapy and adaptive horsemanship programs. They can include physical therapists, occupational therapists, speech therapists, psychologists, certified riding instructors, and others. Those who provide equine-assisted therapy must go to school to study and learn the skills they will need to help people. Then, they must pass a test and get a license that will allow them to provide therapy. Most therapists who become involved with therapy horses have had a lot of experience with horses throughout their lives.

Riding instructors must also have special training. They must learn how to teach riding to people with special needs while a mentor, a trusted teacher, watches them. Then, they must give an example of their teaching and take a test to become certified. Being certified means the riding instructor has the knowledge and skills that PATH requires.

The horses themselves must also be trained. Before horses are accepted by Mane Stream, they are tested to make sure they have the right personality and movement to be useful to the program. After they arrive, they are exposed to all kinds of things, such as balls, rings, noisy toys, and hula hoops, that might be used in therapy or riding sessions to make sure they do not get nervous or spook.

Next, the horses are introduced to the mounting process, including the mechanical lift. Then, they are ridden by a trainer. She makes sure the horses understand the types of cues, or signs, participants may give. Some riders are very noisy, so the trainer also makes sure the horses will not be upset by yelling or unexpected screams. Other participants easily become unbalanced, so the horses must get used to this feeling too. The trainer also makes sure the horses can work with side walkers next to them. The next step is to try trail riding to see how the horses react. Therapy horses must always be calm. They must also have good manners while being led and handled in the barn.

Therapy horses are trained to remain calm while participants mount and volunteers surround them.

Chapter 5

Groundwork With Therapy Horses

Therapy horses were originally used to help people overcome physical challenges, such as injuries or disabilities. But over time, it became very clear that horses provide other benefits as well. People in these programs were calmer and happier. They did not even have to be riding the horses. Just being around the horses made people feel better.

Another group formed, the Equine Assisted Growth and Learning Association (EAGALA), which offers two programs. One of the programs, called equine-assisted psychotherapy, helps people with emotional problems. The other program, equine-assisted learning, helps people learn how to get along with others at their jobs.

FAST FACT

Miniature horses help people too! They visit people who may be lonely in nursing homes, assisted-living centers, and hospitals. Just petting and talking to the animals can make the residents feel happy. Miniature horses that are part of animal-assisted therapy programs have to be specially trained and certified as well.

Spring Reins of Hope is a member of EAGALA and offers sessions in New York and New Jersey. All of the exercises are performed with the person on the ground directing the horse. One example of an equine-assisted psychotherapy exercise is called "Pick Out a Horse and Tell Him/Her a Secret." When someone talks about things that bother him, he often feels more relaxed. The participant feels safe sharing things with the horse because the horse will not get mad at him or tell the secret to anybody. The horse will be a true friend and only listen.

Working with horses in this way helps people make good changes in themselves and their relationships. Children's schoolwork improves, and they have an easier time dealing with people. They can feel happy again after bad experiences or improve their relationships with their families. Adults even get along better with each other at work.

A little boy talks to a horse at Spring Reins of Hope. Horses are good listeners for people who have trouble communicating with others.

How do horses create all these wonderful changes? Because they are large, powerful animals, people can be afraid of them. So when horses respond to our commands, it builds our confidence and helps us get over our fears. Horses do not care about what we look like or what problems we have, just how we act when we are with them. And like us, they enjoy being around their own kind, are curious, and like to have fun.

"Recently we had sessions with a young boy, about eleven years old, who had anger outbursts," says Christina, the founder of Spring Reins of Hope. "Allowing him to spend some time connecting with our Thoroughbred mare, who is very sensitive to attitude and mood changes, helped him to see and realize for himself that others are affected by our actions. After two visits with the horse he stated, 'Working with the horses is pretty cool. I never thought a horse could sense all of that.'"

Michelle takes a ride on the author's horse, Elwood, while the author walks beside them. Elwood is a very special friend to both Michelle and the author.

Spring Reins of Hope uses different types of horses for different kinds of groups. One special horse is brought in when bullying is the problem. As soon as someone acts in a way meant to frighten the horse, the horse himself will become difficult too. So within minutes, all the participants try to find a nicer way to complete their activities with the horses.

There is something wonderful about being on the ground and looking into the eyes of a horse. And some often have an especially gentle look that horse lovers call "a kind eye." The author's horse, Elwood, is one of them. "When I look into El's eyes I feel a strong connection to him. He is a very calm horse and helps me relax. I do not always have to ride him. Just spending time with him always makes me feel good," the author says.

When Therapy Horses Retire

As you can see, therapy horses are very special animals. Because of their gentle personalities, affection for people, helpful movements, and willingness to cooperate, they improve the lives of countless people with physical and emotional challenges. The bond that develops between a participant and her therapy horse is truly unique. It can make the participant's life better in so many ways.

A girl kisses a horse after her equine-assisted therapy session. People develop special bonds with the horses that help them overcome the difficulties in their lives.

But there will come a time when most therapy horses will need to retire. They may become too old to comfortably carry people on their backs. Or they may have health problems that would make it difficult for them to keep working. So where do these horses go when they retire? Some may be adopted by local families and live out their lives as pets. Because horses are herd animals, they always like to live with at least one horse friend. Others may go to large horse retirement farms where they live with many other older horses, wandering

FAST FACT

A horse can live for about twenty to thirty-five years.

through large pastures, eating grass, and simply enjoying themselves. They certainly deserve this easy life after giving many years of special service to the people who have needed them the most.

Glossary

adaptive riding—A therapeutic riding program where the person moves the horse.

carriage driving—An activity in which the participant drives a horse-drawn cart.

certified—Proven to have the knowledge and skills to do a specific job.

draft horse—A heavy breed of horse originally used for farmwork.

equine-assisted therapy—A therapeutic program where the horse moves the person.

hand—A unit of measurement equal to four inches used to measure the height of a horse from the hooves to the withers.

high-spirited—Energetic; bold; enthusiastic.

interactive vaulting—A program that can be either equine-assisted therapy or adaptive riding where the participant makes movements around, on, and off the horse.

Glossary

license—Legal permission to do something.

mechanical lift—A machine that helps people mount a horse.

mentor—An experienced and trusted teacher.

occupational therapy—A type of therapy that helps people who have trouble doing everyday tasks, such as getting dressed, taking a shower, or brushing their teeth, because of an illness, injury, or disability.

participant—A person in a therapeutic riding program.

psychotherapy—Treatment of mental or emotional problems.

side walker—A person who walks beside a rider on a horse to make sure she does not fall off.

tacking up—Placing riding equipment, such as the saddle, bridle, stirrups, and reins, on a horse.

withers—The tallest point on a horse's body; it is located between the shoulders.

Learn More

Books

Marsico, Katie. *Therapy Horses.* New York: Marshall Cavendish, 2013.

Murray, Julie. *Therapy Animals.* Edina, Minn.: Buddy Books, 2009.

Nagle, Jeanne. *Working Horses.* New York: Gareth Stevens Pub., 2011.

Nichols, Catherine. *Therapy Horses.* New York: Bearport Pub. Co., 2007.

Internet Addresses

American Humane Association
<http://www.americanhumane.org>

Professional Association of Therapeutic Horsemanship (PATH) International
<http://www.pathintl.org>

Equine Assisted Growth and Learning Association (EAGALA)
<http://www.eagala.org>

Index